WORK FROM HOME & MAKE 6-FIGURES

The JOY of Making More in Half the Time

Without the Hassles of a Job, Boss, or Commute

MICHELLE KULP

Table of Contents

Imagine working fewer hours; a lot fewer hours.

Imagine working only those hours that fit in with what you really want to do every day – instead of having to force your life around your work schedule.

Imagine being able to work from anywhere you choose – locally, nationally or internationally.

Imagine doubling or tripling your income.

You don't have to imagine it any longer; it can be a reality.

Introduction

I have a confession to make…

I am ambitiously lazy.

Sounds like an oxymoron, right? *Ambitious* and *lazy* in the same sentence?

Let me explain.

When I was a teenager, I loved going to the bookstore and buying "Home-based Business" magazines to research all the different ways to *make money without having a job.*

I imagined one day being my own boss, making my own hours, controlling my money and time…and of course, working from home.

I was born with an entrepreneurial spirit, and over the years, I've had several businesses such as:

- Roommate Matching Service

- Private Process Service

- Personalized Children's Books Publisher

- Public Speaking Facilitator

- Career Coach

- Network marketing companies including PartyLite, Christmas Around the World, and North American Power.

- Cleaning Company
- Crafts
- Babysitting Services
- Resume Writing Service
- And More!

What I realized after having all these businesses is that deep down, what I really wanted was *to make the most amount of money with the least amount of time.*

I think being *ambitiously lazy* is about being smart with your time.

Timothy Ferriss, author of the #1 New York Times Bestseller, *The 4-Hour Workweek,* says *"…the perfect job is the one that takes the least time."*

After graduating college in 1983, I had a 17-year traditional 9-to-5 career as a paralegal, and at the end of those 17 years I was working 40+ hours per week making $48,000 per year living paycheck-to-paycheck. The only way I could make more money was to work more hours.

I hated the fact that I had to trade time for money.

After my legal career ended, I began creating multiple streams of income as well as passive income streams. I loved trying out new things to see if I liked them and I also loved not depending on one source of income as I had for so many years.

I was fortunate enough to find a job in outside sales and within eighteen months, I was making six figures working only

20-25 hours per week! I didn't even know making six figures was possible or that I could earn that much and cut my work time in half.

I learned so much working in sales, and I love teaching others that it is possible to make six figures without selling your soul.

I started my first website www.becomea6figurewoman.com in 2005 and I sold online courses for $197. Within my first 30 days, I made $2,500 and I was hooked.

I loved working from home as well as the concept of doing the work once and getting paid over and over!

The online world has changed drastically since 2005 and it's not as easy to make six figures from an online course like I was doing back then without spending a lot of money on paid advertising, copywriting and sales funnels. Plus, there is a lot more competition than there was in 2005.

At the time, I sold mostly to people that were on a small email list which I built from doing live workshops

The 6-week online courses were very simple: no videos, just a PDF and weekly calls.

I really enjoyed developing new programs and teaching them to others.

Over the years, I've made money online in a variety of ways such as:

- Royalties from my books
- Copywriting

- Website Design
- SEO
- Coaching
- Selling Online Courses
- Bestselling Author Program (done-for-you)
- Ghostwriting
- Sales
- Affiliate Income

After my 17-year career in the legal field ended, I worked in outside sales selling hot tubs in-home for 10 years until the company I was working for filed bankruptcy in 2010. I had to make a decision since my cushy 6-figure job was disappearing. At the time, my online business was generating anywhere between $3000 to $5000 per month part-time in a feast or famine rollercoaster mode; I desperately needed to make six figures online or I would have to go back to a dreaded "job."

The thought of going back to a job after being away from one for so long literally made me sick to my stomach. I would do anything to not have to go back to the corporate grind.

This book focuses on exactly what I did to take my side hustle earning $3-$5k per month to $25k+ per month consistently.

I'll also share the mistakes I made along the way, so you can be aware of them and not make the same ones.

I'm going to share with you everything I've done to create an amazing business and lifestyle getting paid to do what I love and having the freedom to work from home.

My online business gives me three reasons to jump out of bed in the morning:

1. Total autonomy

2. Creativity

3. Great work/life balance

I can barely tell the difference between work and pleasure.

If it's your dream to work from home while only working 20-25 hours a week or less, to earn six figures (or multiple six figures) doing what you love so you can have time and money freedom...you're in the right place!

Let's get started!

Chapter 1:
Wealth in a Wheelchair

To trade time is to trade life.

One of my favorite books is *The Millionaire Fastlane* by MJ DeMarco. In his book, he talks about three barriers to wealth:

- Get Rich Slow

- The Slow Lane

- Wealth in a Wheelchair

Many people believe that you "Go to school, get good grades, graduate, get a good job, save 10%, invest in the stock market, max your 401k, slash your credit cards, and clip coupons…then someday, when you are, oh, 65 years old, you will be rich."

Like many others, I followed down this flawed path, but at the end of my 17-year legal career, I was broke, living paycheck-to-paycheck, had less than one year's salary in my 401k, and was struggling financially.

I was on a hamster wheel and I could not see an end in sight.

I did everything I was supposed to do. I graduated from college, got a good job with great benefits, put as much as I could afford to into my 401k, clipped coupons, lived frugally, but as a single mom with three kids living in a high-cost metropolitan area, it was not working.

The message of "Get Rich Slow" is that you have to sacrifice your today, your dreams, and your life for a plan that pays dividends after your life has passed you by.

I don't know about you, but I don't want *wealth in wheelchair*. I want to enjoy life now.

I've known many people who retire and then pass away a short time after. We don't know how long we have in this life, so why wait until the golden years of retirement to have wealth. The real golden years are when you're younger, more energetic and vibrant.

I'm 56 years old now and when I left my corporate job, I was 37. I didn't have a plan; all I knew was the 9-to-5 grind was not working for me and I needed a change.

As fate would have it, I was given a pink slip from the law firm where I worked and that was the golden ticket to a new life.

I had zero dollars in the bank and three young kids to support.

In my book, *How to Find Your Passion: 23 Questions that Can Change Your Entire Life*, I talk about a chance meeting I had with Billy Ray Cyrus. He asked me a question that changed the trajectory of my life: "What are your Dreams?" My reply at the time was, "I don't have any dreams, my life is about survival."

I was living paycheck-to-paycheck and didn't have time to think about things like dreams.

(Billy Ray and me, circa October 23, 1992)

Billy Ray assured me that everyone has a dream and he made me promise that I would look for my dream and never ever give up on my dream once I found it.

I spent a year searching for this elusive dream that Billy Ray talked about. Ironically, I found the answer through another question.

I was at the bookstore browsing the self-help section when *How to Find Your Mission In Life* by Richard Bolles literally fell into my hands. In that book, Bolles asked, *"What do you love to do where you lose all sense of time?"*

The only thing I could recall was in my younger years, I loved writing—essays, reports, short stories, poems, and more. I never thought about writing as my passion, but looking back,

I realized my favorite part of my job as a paralegal was legal writing and research.

Equipped with the knowledge that *writing* was my passion, I started down the path to becoming a newspaper reporter to gain some writing experience. Then, I started my own blog and wrote blog posts, online courses, website content, and of course, books.

I loved NOT trading my time for money and instead, I focused on different ways to leverage my time.

Having a job is like being on a hamster wheel – you can never get off because they voraciously consume your time.

If you work, you get paid. If you don't work, you don't get paid.

Many people with 9-to-5 jobs talk about 'job security,' but the job market is constantly evolving. Jobs are rapidly disappearing because of new technology. Companies are able to hire contractors globally with no overhead costs. I'm sure you know several people in your life (maybe you) that unexpectedly received a pink slip. Job security is a myth.

A job is a prison that takes away your freedom, your control, forces you to work with people you may not like or respect, forces you to get paid last, and has massive restrictions on your income. You are basically trading five days of life for two days of freedom.

That doesn't sound like a good trade to me.

Tim Ferris talks about the *deferred-life plan* that so many people settle for.

Statistics show that 75-85% of employees are extremely unhappy with their jobs.

Mark Twain once said, "Whenever you find yourself on the side of the majority, it is time to pause and reflect."

That time is now.

Don't accept the status quo, and don't waste 10-30 years of your life doing soul-crushing work just because it is the default path.

There is another way.

One year vs. 17 years

Last year, I got a call from one of my youngest clients and authors, Alex, asking if I was still looking for a project manager for my www.bestsellingauthorprogram.com business. "Yes," I replied, "Do you know anyone?"

"Me!"

I was shocked to hear this as Alex had graduated from Virginia Tech with a Bachelor's degree in programming. He took a 6-figure job for a large IT company straight out of college, and from the outside looking in, he was living an amazing life.

Except he wasn't.

He felt trapped in a cubicle.

Alex is a people person who was stuck in a project job, trading time for money.

He did that job for one year and decided he'd had *enough*. He quit his 6-figure job to travel the world, and now he works as my project manager virtually from all over the world.

I look at Alex and wonder why it took me 17 years to break free from job prison when it took Alex only one year? But I was raised in a different generation with a different mindset about jobs and our future.

If you want to read the details of how I broke free from job prison, and read the step-by-step process in my book *Quit Your Job and Follow Your Dreams.*

One of the goals in this book is to help you create wealth fast instead of the default "wealth in wheelchair" approach; it's a simple system to generate cash without consuming time.

Of course, my business does consume some of my time, but my time is much more leveraged than it ever was when I had a job. Most importantly, I choose when I work, where I work, and with whom I work. I'm also able to generate multiple six-figure streams of income which allows me to save six figures per year. We will talk more about that in an upcoming chapter.

Now, let's talk about the *end of jobs* as we know them.

Chapter 2:
The End of Jobs

In the book, *The End of Jobs*, by Taylor Pearson, he says:

"Today, a $40 internet connection and a free Skype account gives anyone access to the greatest talent pool in history. Instead of competing against the labor pool of a few hundred thousand or a few million people in your area near you for your job, you're competing against seven billion people around the world."

Ouch! Seven billion people are your competition.

It's tough to get a job, even a low-skill, low-paying job. The competition is fierce.

I remember the days when you could walk into a business, fill out an application and speak to someone about a job on the same day. That face-to-face connection and interaction has been replaced with technology, and it's very impersonal.

Years ago, when I was in outside sales, I watched my manager throw 80% of incoming resumes that were flowing out of the fax machine at about 6-8 pages per minute directly into the trash can.

I couldn't understand how he decided which resumes to keep and which ones to toss with only a 5-second glance, but he said he knew what he was looking for and he could tell immediately if the applicants were qualified or not.

I'm sure some of those resumes were from qualified people, but they were poorly organized and did not accurately reflect the candidate's experience and qualifications.

In fact, my resume was the reason I got called in for an interview. During the interview, my manager said to me, "You had the best resume of anyone I've ever seen in all my years in business." That was a great compliment!

I had copywriting and sales skills and knew how to grab their attention.

But the point is, it's extremely competitive now in the job market, especially for the higher paying jobs, and it's difficult to get a face-to-face interview without doing something extraordinary to stand out.

Plus, you're competing with people around the world who can do many of the jobs available and are willing to do it for a fraction of the cost.

Skill-Stacking is the Next Best Thing

After I left the corporate world, I figured out very quickly that in order to be marketable and sought after, I needed to learn new skills that were in high demand.

I call this *skill-stacking,* and it's the best way to increase your value in the marketplace—especially if you want to work from home and make six figures.

The first skill I decided to focus on when I started my on-line business was copywriting. I remember reading all those "Home-Based Business" magazines and the persuasive writing that made me want to sign up for whatever they were selling.

I was fortunate to connect with a local copywriter legend in my area named Yanik Silver. I was his student for many years and that's where I learned the art of copywriting. I knew that one skill would separate me from the competition.

Joe Vitale, in his book, *Hypnotic Writing: How to Seduce and Persuade Customers with Only Your Words*, says,

"There are three keys to the success of any direct marketing campaign, whether it's done online or off:

1. The list

2. The offer

3. The copy"

I knew copywriting was a skill that would pay off so I started as a student and learned everything I could about it until I mastered it.

Robert Collier, one of the most well-known copywriters in the world, said, "Your problem, then, is to find a point of contact with his (the reader's) interests, his desires, some feature that will flag his attention and make your letter stand out from all the others the moment he reads the first line."

Because I was a litigation Paralegal, I knew about the power of persuasion to win legal cases. It made sense to me that you could have a beautiful website, but if you had subpar copywriting, you would probably be broke because you couldn't convert visitors to sales.

Mastering copywriting paid off for me because it gave me the ability to write sales letters, emails, ads, and blog posts to sell courses and programs. Others would pay me for copywriting services and I started out charging $997 for a long copy sales letter.

I'm sharing this with you because the more skills you can learn and become proficient at, the more options and value you have out in the competitive world.

The second skill I learned was sales, and that has paid off 10x! If you have a business and can't sell, then you'll probably be a broke business owner. So, you'll either need to learn how to make sales or hire someone who is a master at it.

In addition to copywriting and sales, I developed the following skills over the years that pay me dividends still to this day:

- Website Design
- Search Engine Optimization
- Publishing
- Cover Design
- Book Launches
- Writing books
- Sales Calls
- I'm also an expert (self-taught) at a variety of software programs such as Aweber, Hootsuite, Leadpages, Amazon KDP and more

What skills do you have that others would pay you to do, or what skills would you like to learn and then get paid for?

When I see people who are unemployed or stuck in a lower paying jobs, I know they haven't taken the time to develop new skillsets.

Skills pays the bills!

The more skills you have, the more money you can make.

One of the first ways I made money online was writing and selling online courses. Then, I added coaching to provide more personalized services. I also did website design, SEO, copywriting, and eventually started publishing and launching books for myself and others. As a result, I now have multiple streams of six-figure income.

I attribute all of this to taking that first step in learning new skills and then stacking those skills to create value in the marketplace.

I've also discovered that sometimes you spend a lot of time learning a new software program and then the market shifts and you have a decision to make. You can stay where you are or shift with the market. If you want to be successful, you have to learn to shift quickly because technology changes at the speed of light.

Consider, for example, Borders Bookstore. They were the top bookstore for many years, but they didn't pivot fast enough with the creation of eBooks and eBook readers like the NOOK and Kindle. They thought they could continue selling physical books in stores and still be successful. That decision resulted in them going out of business.

If you don't change, you'll stay broke.

In his book, *Linchpin: Are you Indispensable* by Seth Godin, he says, a linchpin is "An individual who can walk into chaos and create order, someone who can invent, connect, create and make things happen."

Being an entrepreneur is about connecting, creating and re-inventing yourself over and over and over. I don't see it as a negative, I love it! I was bored with most jobs I had after the first month because they were monotonous and there was very little change. That's why you see so many big brands going out of business – they didn't want to change. Look at Toys R Us, Sears, Kmart, Borders Bookstore, and more.

We have to shift the question from "How do I get a job doing that?" to "How can I create a job doing that?"

When people ask me what I do, I usually answer, "I'm in publishing" because when I try to explain my business, they look at me like I'm crazy.

I've created a business that involves books because I love books, I love creating content, I love teaching, and I love helping authors succeed. I get paid to do what I love, and that happened because I *created* it.

If I went to any job website, I'm positive I could never find a "Job" that involves doing what I do making multiple six figures. It doesn't exist.

So, instead of looking for a job, create the perfect job using skills you already have (or quickly learn new ones) that are in high demand.

Recently, my former business coach sent out an email to his list stating his business was growing by leaps and bounds and he needed a sales enrollment coach to sell his program.

He spends about $1 million per year on Facebook ads and has a highly targeted and successful coaching business. It's so successful that he can't handle all the strategy session applications he receives.

When I saw his email, I reached out to him and he hired me! A one hour call = $1000!

Why?

Because I mastered the skill of selling on a phone call many years ago. Now, I can use that skill to generate another stream of income in my business.

We will talk more about how to generate multiple six-figure streams of income in an upcoming chapter.

This chapter was about skill-stacking to add value to the marketplace. It's a great place to start.

Next up we are going to talk about your expertise...and how to cash in on it!

Chapter 3:
How to Cash In On Your Expertise

In a blog post by author, speaker and teacher, Seth Godin he wrote:

"Skill vs. Talent

You're born with talent.

You earn a skill.

I don't think there are many situations where talent is the key driver of success. The biggest exception might be that a drive to acquire skill could be a talent...

Assuming you have even once done the hard work to learn something important, then you have what you need to develop even more skills.

Go do that.

We need generosity and passion. And even more so, we need people who care to develop the skills to deliver on their promises."

There a few things we need to talk about.

Some people have natural born talents that they cash in on and others learn skills that they cash in on. And some do both.

Either way, you can use your existing skill set to build a lucrative business that earns six figures while working from home or you can take your natural talents, add some new skills, and do the same.

I was born with a natural talent for writing, but I still had to learn different aspects of writing such as copywriting, storytelling, editing, formatting, publishing, and more.

To cash in on your expertise, answer these questions:

- What do people tell me I'm good at? Is there a high demand for this in the marketplace?

- What obstacles and problems have I overcome in my life? Could I help others do the same? Is there a high demand for this in the marketplace?

- What am I an expert at already? Is there a high demand for this in the marketplace?

- What skills can I learn that interest me and is there a high demand for those in the marketplace?

Answering these questions is a good place to start.

We are all experts at many things, and some areas of expertise are very unique. Years ago, I read a story about a couple who paid zero dollars for their groceries because they had an extraordinary coupon clipping talent. They started a blog and charged others to teach them to do the same.

Sounds crazy, right?

I want you to list ten things you are an expert at that you think you might be able to charge for:

1. _____

2. _____

3. _____

4. _____

5. _____

6. _____

7. _____

8. _____

9. _____

10. _____

In my bestselling author program and business, I use all of the skills listed below to make six figures:

- Sales
- Copywriting/Writing
- Editing
- Formatting
- Cover Design
- Project Management
- Amazon Categories and Keywords Research

- Book Launches
- Networking
- Speaking

I developed this skill set over time; it didn't happen overnight.

The more skills you can combine, the more money you will make!

My good friend, Jackie Woodside, was a Licensed Clinical Social Worker for many years. She was very successful, but eventually got burned out in this field. She decided to reinvent herself and became a certified Life Coach.

Jackie loves creating curriculum and eventually created her signature "Life Design" coaching program. She took that business to six figures using her existing skill set and adding new skills to that.

Once her coaching business was successful, she added a training program and certifies coaches on her methodology for her Life Design program. Today, she has a thriving multiple six-figure coaching and training business.

In an upcoming chapter, we will be talking about the 6-figure blueprint I learned from my business coach that turned my business from a side-hustle to a thriving 6-figure business. And we will also be talking about how to create multiple six-figure income streams.

Once your first 6-figure business is up and running, there is usually some aspect of that business that you can turn into another 6-figure stream of income.

Right now you might be asking, "What expertise could I use to create a 6-figure business?"

Let's change the question to this:

"What expertise do I have right now that I could use to make my first $1000?"

This small shift in the question doesn't make it feel so overwhelming.

First, test it to see if there is a market for what you are selling. Then, see how you feel about it after you've made your first $1000 doing it. You might discover that you didn't like it that much after all.

After you make your first $1000, you can easily shift gears because you are not that heavily invested in the business.

The mistake I continually see people make is investing thousands of dollars on a website, branding, logos, sales funnels, creating online courses, etc. only to find out it doesn't work and no one is buying what they're selling. Now, their confidence is down and they feel stuck because they've spent so much money.

Don't make this mistake!

The foreword of *The 7-Day Startup* by Dan Norris says:

"Without question, the biggest mistake people make is obsessing over their idea and not focusing enough on finding people willing to pay for their product."

One of my favorite chapters in this book is "*You Don't Learn Until You Launch.*" It's fun to build a website, pick your brand colors and designs, get a logo done, work on the copyrighting, develop a program, talk about your business, etc.

The problem is there's an imbalance - you're spending too much time on an unproven idea. You need to have sales to prove your idea is worth pursuing.

Execution is your ability to present an idea and get customers to pay for that idea and that is all that matters.

Dan Norris wrote this book because he invested 7+ years in a business that failed and he learned what NOT to do.

Here's what WANNAPRENEURS focus on:

- Building expensive websites
- Optimizing their site
- New life-changing ideas
- Logos
- Branding
- Photoshoots
- Sales Funnels
- Expensive courses
- Reading books
- Listening to podcasts
- Talking endlessly about their idea
- Attending events endlessly

They do everything except get customers!

If you have a natural talent or a skill set and you want to test it out, I highly recommend you do it quickly. Don't spend hundreds or thousands of dollars on the tasks listed above. Instead, create a minimum viable product (MVP) and launch it.

You can launch your MVP without a website or expensive sales funnels.

If you want a roadmap for doing this, then pick up a copy of *The 7-Day Startup* by Dan Norris. It's a great book!

And remember this from Dan Norris:

"It's amazing what you can achieve in 7 days. You can't deliver on your whole grand vision, but you can launch something. When you do, you can start talking to people who are paying you money. This is when you start making sensible business decisions and avoid assumptions."

I'm telling you this because I made this mistake in 2004 before I launched my first website, Become a 6-Figure Woman. I spent thousands of dollars I didn't have on a website that didn't work, and I wasted an excessive amount of time choosing colors, images, branding, etc.

Looking back, it was my own fear of launching that was causing me to get bogged down in research and I mistakenly felt like I was *busy* working on my business, when, in reality, I was just wasting time.

An MVP is something you can launch in seven days. Sounds crazy, but Dan is right. Don't waste your time on expensive

Facebook ads if you don't have any paying customers for that product or service.

When I hired my business coach who turned my business around and tripled my income in 90 days, he told me never to run Facebook ads until you have a proven offer that converts.

Many people think the answer to all their business problems is Facebook ads, but they don't have a proven offer that converts.

You can test ideas and offers with a simple landing page before building a complete website.

I had the ugliest business website for years and I still made six figures year after year. The colors were bad, I had no logo, no style, etc., but at the end of the day, the only thing that mattered was the sales copy, the calls to action, and that my offer converted.

I have a client who is a Master Coach for The Life Coach School and I'm amazed at the types of niche' coaches who have successful businesses:

- Binge Eating Coach
- Real Estate Coach
- Weight Loss Coach
- Autoimmune Coach
- Feminist Confidence Coach
- Money Coach
- Mindfulness Coach
- Menopause Coach

- Running Coach
- The Deep Dive Coach (one of my clients)
- Female Entrepreneur Coach
- Non-Profit Career Coach
- Adoption Coach
- Introvert Coach
- Stop Over-Drinking Coach

So, when people tell me "I'm not an expert"…that's a lie. You are an expert at many things. I'm certain you've overcome problems, and that right there makes you an expert.

Think of it this way. We are all on a path and some people are further ahead of us in different areas and some are behind us. You are an expert to the people who are further behind you on the path.

Right now, some people are making $1000 per month from their online business. I am making $25k+ per month, so I am further along that they are, which means I am an expert and I can help them.

Have you ever heard the saying "Make your Mess Your Message"? What messes can you turn into a message to help others?

And if you aren't interested in doing that, then focus on your skills, developing new skills, and using your existing natural talents.

Now that we've talked about how to cash in on your expertise, next we are going to talk about the "sampling" stage.

Chapter 4:
Sample First, Select Second

I hired my business coach in September 2014. He took one look at my website and said "Michelle, what is all this stuff? We need to pick one thing and focus on that one thing."

He was absolutely right. At the time, I was selling a variety of online courses such as:

- Quit Your Job and Follow Your Dreams
- How to Start a Profitable Blog
- Creating Online Courses that Sell
- How to Write a Mission Statement
- 6-Figure Woman

I wasn't making a lot of money from one thing. I was making a little money from a lot of things.

I started my online business in 2005 and it was my part-time side hustle. I had a 6-figure outside sales job from 2004 until 2010, so I had another source of income that paid the bills and wasn't completely reliant on my online business.

Once that 6-figure sales job ended, however, I really needed to turn my side hustle into my 6-figure business so I hired a business coach.

Even though picking one thing to focus on in my business was brilliant and it catapulted me to six figures, when you're first starting out, it is a good idea to have a *sampling period.*

As we talked about in the previous chapter, you want to create a minimum viable product and launch in a short period of time—ideally 7 days, max-30 days.

Ideas are a dime a dozen. It's the execution that's hard and you don't learn until you execute the idea. So, you won't know if you really like it until you actually do it.

A Cool Way to Sample

There is a website called Pivot Planet (formerly named Vocation Vacations) that allows you to find someone who is doing the job you want to do and consult with them to "test drive your dream job". I love that idea!

Check it out at:

https://www.pivotplanet.com/

Enter a description for the type of career or business you want to work in and find an advisor that you can consult with and ask questions about. Here are some featured advisor careers:

- Voiceover Artist
- Blogger
- Filmmaker
- Technology Entrepreneur
- Airbnb host

- Marketing Firm Owner
- Professional Speaker
- Publisher
- Radio Personality
- Web Developer
- Online Course Creator

You can view the full list of advisors here: https://www.pivotplanet.com/browse.

I recommend hiring an advisor so you can see if this is something you really want to do and learn the good, the bad and the ugly about it.

Working from home and making six figures sounds great, but the devil is in the details.

The biggest mistake people make is investing too much time, money and resources before making a dime on their business or idea.

Don't make that mistake. Do your due diligence. Hire an advisor and ask questions. If it's something that still interests you, then create your minimum viable product and make your first $1000. If you still love it after that, then you have the green light to invest more of your money, time and energy into it.

Looking back, it was important for me to "sample" different ways to make money.

I've made money online in dozens of ways, and some of them I liked and some I did not.

Here's an example of something I tried that I did not like:

At the time, I noticed some people were recommending having a year-long program. A year sounded like a long time to me, so I launched a 6-month program instead. Six months to a year is a long time to work with people. I found when there is a shorter amount of time like 6-12 weeks, you get better results with people because there is more motivation to complete tasks when there is a tighter deadline.

I did that 6-month coaching program one time and it was very lucrative. Six people paid $1000 a month for six months so I made $36,000, but it wasn't really something that I absolutely loved doing so I never offered it again.

You must make money and get your first clients before you will ever know if you really enjoy it.

When my son graduated high school, he told me he wanted to be a massage therapist and the tuition was $10,000 for him to get certified. It sounded like a good idea, but my gut told me he needed to actually *experience* it.

I had a good friend who was a licensed massage therapist working out of her home. I set an appointment for my son to have a one-hour massage and afterwards, he would sit down and talk to her about the business side of things when they were done.

I waited out in the car because I didn't want to influence him. About 90 minutes later, my son came to the car and said, "I could never do that to people. I definitely don't want to be a massage therapist."

Thank God I listened to my intuition because that would have been a $10,000 mistake!

A lot of things sound exciting or sexy or lucrative, but until you know the details involved on the back-end, it might be an illusion and not something you truly enjoy.

In my book, *Quit Your Job and Follow Your Dreams*, I include a chapter that shows readers how to do a job autopsy.

Do Your Own Job Autopsy

I suggest going through all of your previous jobs (and current job if you are working) and writing down all the daily tasks you do and then rate those on a scale of 1-10 to see what you love and what you don't.

It's an eye-opening experience because most people who hate their jobs are spending 75% of their time on tasks they hate or dislike and only 25% on tasks they love.

When it comes to creating your own 6-figure business, you want to make sure you're spending 75% of your time on tasks you love and only 25% or less on tasks you don't love.

Of course, you can outsource the tasks you don't love, but it's important to be realistic about what is involved in the type of business you're looking to start.

My online business involves a lot of technology, learning new software, understanding algorithms, research, writing, typing, talking to people, reading manuscripts, managing book projects, etc.

When I first started www.bestsellingauthorprogram.com in 2013, I was doing everything in my business. I was literally a solopreneur. Fast forward now to my business and I worked with a talented team of people:

- Cover Designer
- Editor
- Formatter
- Amazon Ads Expert
- Project Manager
- Proof-reader
- Virtual Assistant

It was hard letting go of the reins, but eventually you have to pick the one or two things you're great at and laser focus on those things.

Go through the list of expert advisors on Pivot Plant and select the top three areas in which you would like to make six figures while working from home.

Go to: https://www.pivotplanet.com/browse

My top three choices for making six figures from home:

1. _____

2. _____

3. _____

Next, talk to at least one successful person who is doing what you want to do and ask them the following ten questions:

1. Does this job have the potential to make six figures?

2. How many hours do you spend on your business per week?

3. What do you love about your business?

4. What do you hate about your business?

5. What have you learned since you started this business that you wish you knew before you started?

6. Do I need any special training to do this and if so, what would you recommend?

7. How many years did it take you to become successful?

8. What advice would you give to someone like me who is just starting out?

9. What were the three biggest mistakes you made in this business?

10. If you could do things over, would you choose this business?

This will give you a good gauge on if this is really something you want to pursue.

If the business involves a lot of sitting at the computer, and you prefer to be outdoors, maybe that's not for you.

Performing a job autopsy and talking with an expert advisor will save you tons of time, money, and energy going down the wrong path.

Once you've done this, and you feel good about what you've learned then by all means, get started.

I have a good friend, James, who works in IT and has decided he wants more time and money freedom. He is currently enrolled in the Life Design Coaching training program I mentioned earlier and he plans to transition to a full-time Life Design Coach in the next year.

James did his due diligence before jumping in and knows what is involved in starting a life coaching business. The great part is, James has technology skills which he will need to get his business off the ground.

It does take money to make money.

I recommend keeping your day job and only leaving once you have enough money in the bank to cover one year's expenses, you have no debt, and you've made your first $1000 in your new line of business.

Of course, there are no guarantees. My income was feast or famine for many years which is why I kept my 6-figure outside sales job. I also loved sales and I loved driving to appointments and meeting new people. So that worked for me.

You can also consider going from full-time to part-time work while you build up your new business. Then, when you are financially ready, you can take the leap!

Now that we've talked about sampling and trying things out, next up we are going to talk about going deep and not wide.

Chapter 5:
Go Deep, Not Wide

There are different seasons of a business. When you are starting out, it's important to *sample* things to see what you like. I always recommend making your first $1000 from your selected business model by doing a 7-day or maximum 30-day launch.

After you complete your sampling period, which could be as long as a year, then it's time to go deep, not wide.

I have another confession to make...

I am a recovering 'Shiny New Objects' chaser! It's so much fun in the beginning when you're learning something new with so many exciting possibilities. However, in the beginning you are really looking at whatever "it" is through rose-colored glasses.

This approach worked well when I was in the sampling period, but it doesn't work well in the long term or enable you to build a sustainable six-figure business.

If you're like me, and you like to do a little on a lot of things, it can be difficult to choose one thing.

The Lesson I Learned at Five Years Old

When I was five years old (circa, 1968), my dad took me to the toy store on Christmas Eve to buy presents for me and my three brothers. It was late and the store was closing soon so we had limited time. He took me to the doll aisle and said, "Michelle, you can have any doll you want, just pick one out and I'll be back in a few minutes." He left me on my own to select my "one" doll while he shopped for gifts for my brothers. (Back then, you could leave your child in a store unattended and it was safe. Times have changed!)

When my dad came back to the doll aisle, he found me kneeling on the floor crying with about 10 dolls laid out in front of me. "Michelle, if you don't pick one doll, you're going home with no doll!"

Unfortunately, I couldn't pick one. I wanted them all. And guess what? I went home with NO doll.

The moral of the story is we need to pick one thing and then master that because that's where the big money is. When you become the go-to expert in your field for that "one thing," then the money starts flowing in.

My business coach made me pick one thing to focus on and I thankfully I chose my www.bestsellingauthorprogram.com business because I love books and I love working with authors. It turned my entire business around and within 90 days, I was making six figures! In fact, I had my first $22,000 month because of his advice. And every year my income soars!

I'm not going to lie. It's hard to stay in one lane. I see so many things I want to do, but if I take energy away from my bestselling author program business, then that income will most likely decrease.

I have become a go-to person in this niche' and every year I easily add on new income streams in this business.

Malcolm Gladwell talks about working on something for 10,000 hours to get to the level of mastery. If you want to make six figures from home, then you need to become a master of "one thing" and do it so well that there is no competition.

To Quit or Not to Quit

The reason people start things and then quit is because of what bestselling author Seth Godin calls "the dip." In fact, he wrote an entire book about it called *The Dip: A Little Book That Teaches You When To Quit (And When To Stick)* and in it he quotes Vince Lombardi:

"Vince Lombardi: Quitters never win and winners never quit." Godin follows with, "Bad advice. Winners quit all the time. They just quit the right stuff at the right time."

Most people quit. They just don't quit successfully…

Extraordinary benefits accrue to the minority of people who are able to push just a tiny bit longer than most.

Extraordinary benefits also accrue to the tiny majority with the guts to quit early and refocus their efforts on something new.

In both cases, it's about being the best in the world."

So quitting isn't necessarily a bad thing. That's why I suggest sampling different profit paths and then quitting the ones you don't like or are not passionate about.

I've quit a lot of mediocre and passion-less products or services I was selling and I've even given up on ideas about new products or services that I would like to create. Quitting is a huge part of being successful.

A common problem I see, however, is when we invest heavily in something, it's hard to quit. I know because I've done this myself.

For example, let's say you want to be a Life Coach. So you sign up with the Life Coach School and the tuition is around $18,000. Then, you build an amazing website for $5000. Now you need to create a program to sell, so you spend months creating this amazing program (and you have no idea if it will sell). Then, you build an automated webinar and spend thousands of dollars running Facebook ads to it. Maybe you get some clients, or maybe you don't. Finally, you get a few sign ups and start running the program only to realize you don't really like it. The problem is you've invested so much time, energy and resources, that it's hard to quit.

Here's what you can do in the alternative...

Instead of signing up for an $18,000 Life Coaching School, start selling your expertise or services with a simple website or landing page. You can start a Facebook Group and market to the group. Create a blog and drive traffic that way. Create a simple 6-week coaching program with no content (only coaching) and you make your first $1000. Then decide if this is something you want to move forward with. If it is, then you go deeper on it.

Our culture celebrates superstars and winners. We reward the product, book, song, organization or employee that is #1! In fact, it's common for #1 to get ten times the benefit of #10 and a hundred times the benefit of #100.

That's why you want to go deep, not wide, once you select your business profit path so you can become the best at it.

So why does being #1 matter so much?

Because people are short on time and they don't want to take a lot of risks. They would rather head for the person who's ranked best in the world than waste their time doing research and dealing with a mediocre choice.

Also, there's only room at the top for a few, and that creates scarcity. We pay extra for the best, and the best is often scarce.

Scarcity is a result of most people quitting long before they have created something that makes it to the top.

The reason people quit is because of the dip—the long slog between starting and mastery.

In the beginning, any new venture is fun! You're learning new things, it's interesting and stimulating. Then the dip happens which is the "hard work" phase. The long stretch between beginning and true achievement.

The 80/20 rule applies to everything. 80% of the people will never follow through with things they start or dreams they have.

It may sound fun and appear glamorous to be a CEO, but it's a long, hard road to get there and many CEO's spent decades in the dip before landing their high-paying job.

Seth Godin says, "The Dip creates scarcity; scarcity creates value."

So, if you want to make six figures, after you've had your sampling period, then you will go deep, not wide, and you'll whittle through the dip. And when you come out on the other side, you'll be the best in the world.

The dip really is the secret to success.

It's hard to stay on one path.

One day I emailed my coach and said I needed to speak with him right away. I was feeling tired, overworked and burned out even though my 6-figure online business was going well. I was thinking of switching paths.

Thank God I had an amazing coach who helped me work through a few things:

- I needed to outsource more and build a small team. I was stuck in solopreneur mode doing everything in my business and it was draining me.

- I needed to charge more for my done-for-you services.

- I needed to cut back on what I was including in my packages.

I took his advice and it worked.

It was hard for me to let go of the reins and start outsourcing things, but once I did, I wondered why I hadn't done it sooner. First, I hired an editor for my client's books. Then, I hired a world class book designer. Next, a new virtual assistant to set up book launches, and finally, I hired a project manager to keep the business and projects moving and flowing.

Now, it might sound like I have a huge business, but these are all subcontractors who work virtually. They are not employees. Some work a few hours a month or a few hours a day but having this virtual support team has freed up my time so I can work on my special gifts – writing, coaching, sales, and launch strategies.

When I was going through this tough time, my coach asked me, "Michelle, how much do you need to charge to make you want to get out of bed in the morning?"

I thought that was a funny question, but he was right. I was under-charging for my services, so of course I was getting tons of clients as a result. Then, I had to do all this work by myself and it was stressful and tiring. Because I was under-charging, I wasn't feeling motivated to get out of bed in the morning to complete all the projects I was bringing in.

As a result of our call, I increased my price points and created three new packages for authors.

Lastly, I had to remove some of the done-for-you services I was including in my packages. My coach pointed out that I was trying to give clients everything they could possibly need to build a business around a book.

That wasn't sustainable, and it wasn't what my clients were hiring me to do. I was hired to publish and launch a high-quality book to the bestsellers list that my clients could leverage and use in their business and life. So, I eliminated some of the items included in my packages that were outside the original scope of the project.

Once I made those three changes, things got much better. I've been able to free up my time and add on new 6-figure streams of income as a result.

I'm sharing these stories with you because they are real and they are part of the mistakes I made as I built my business. I don't want you to make the same ones.

Here's what we've learned:

- Have a sampling period.
- Be a strategic quitter.
- Pick one thing.
- Go Deep, Not Wide (after the sampling period).
- Move through the Dip.
- Be #1 at your one thing.
- Hire a great business coach to help you navigate around your blind spots.

Next up is a chapter about picking high-hanging fruit to create a sustainable six figure business from home.

Chapter 6:
Pick the High-Hanging Fruit

In his book, *The Pumpkin Plan: A Simple Strategy to Grow a Remarkable Business in any Field*, Mike Michaelowicz says:

"Ordinary pumpkins are always forgotten. Only the giant pumpkin draws a crowd…The giant pumpkin is legend. And when you've grown one…you will be legend too."

Mike uses the analogy of pumpkin farmers who grow half-ton pumpkins as the secret formula to big time entrepreneurial success: "Plant hearty seeds, identify the most promising pumpkins, *kill off the rest of the vine*, and *nurture only the pumpkins with the biggest potential.*"

This chapter is all about finding your most "promising" business idea, then "killing off" the rest of the vine and nurturing only the ones with the biggest potential.

In his Pumpkin Plan book, Mike shares the story of how he owned a computer technology company for four years. He was working 16-18 hours a day, seven days a week and the grind never let up. Although they were doing a million dollars in revenue, there costs were high, the cash flow was not flowing and there was barely any profit.

Mike hired a business coach who helped him turn around his failing million-dollar business that was burning him out, and the first order of business was to *cut his client list.*

In fact, here was his coach's advice:

"List your clients in order of revenue, then take your top-paying clients and separate them into two categories: great clients and everyone else–from the ho-hum clients to the clients who annoy you so much, you cringe when they call you. Keep the great, top-paying clients and cut the rest. Every single one."

Sounds extreme, right?

It was. But guess what? It turned his business around.

Also it turns out that giant pumpkin growers use the same approach with these seven steps:

"Step One: Plant Promising seeds.

Step Two: Water, water, water.

Step Three: As they grow, they routinely REMOVE all of the diseased or damaged pumpkins.

Step Four: WEED like a mad dog. Not a single green leaf or root permitted if it isn't a pumpkin plant.

Step Five: When they grow larger, identify the stronger, faster-growing pumpkins. Then REMOVE all the less promising pumpkins. Repeat until you have one pumpkin on each vine.

Step Six: FOCUS all of your attention on the BIG PUMPKIN. Nurture it around the clock like a baby and guard it like you would your first Mustang convertible.

Step Seven: Watch it grow. In the last days of the season, this will happen so fast you can actually see it happen."

In the previous chapters, we talked about the sampling period, followed up with choosing one thing. Now, it's time to talk about high-ticket clients vs. low ticket clients.

Put your clients into one of two groups:

- **Group 1**: People with an abundance of time who are short on money.

- **Group 2:** People with a shortage of time who have an abundance of money.

When I started my online business in 2005, I worked with people in Group 1. After years of working with this group, I did not have a six-figure business. I was working hard, but not making much progress.

In 2014, when I hired my amazing business coach, he told me to get rid of all my low-paying courses, programs and services and focus on serving Group 2.

The crazy part was, I was afraid to let go of that income so this was a great lesson in trust.

I listened to him and shut everything down even though it was scary and hard. At the same time, I was creating what is now my high-level Bestselling Author Program which focuses on Group 2.

The amazing thing about working with people who are short on time, but who have an abundance of money is that they are very low maintenance. They're a pleasure to work with and they have a professional and business mindset.

Unfortunately, most people go after Group 1 – the low hanging fruit.

Why?

Because it's easier to get low hanging fruit than high hanging fruit.

What people don't understand, though, is that the majority of entrepreneurs and business owners are ALL going after the low hanging fruit, so the competition is tough.

Wouldn't you rather go after the 10% of the market that has money and is willing to invest in a high-ticket program to get the results they are seeking?

Getting back to the seven steps I mentioned earlier that Mike got from his business coach, here's what I did in my business to go from a side hustle to six figures:

- Removed all of my low-ticket programs.
- Focused all of my time and energy on one program – the Bestselling Author Program.
- Weeded out "shiny new objects" and stopped chasing them.
- Identified my top-paying clients and removed the rest.
- Focused all of my attention on my top-paying clients.

I know it sounds enticing to create an online course for $997 and sell dozens or hundreds of copies per month, but it isn't quite as easy as it sounds.

Gone are the days of selling from a sales page on your website. People are much savvier these days and they want high-touch engagement that gets results; the people in Group 2 want a VIP experience.

A $997 price point may sound high to you, but it's not. There are coaches and programs that start at $5000 for eight weeks and go up to $10,000 for a done-with-you program. Done-for-you programs (like mine) have an even higher price point ranging from $8,000 to $25,000+.

The beauty of going for the high-hanging fruit is there is a lot less competition, and you need fewer clients to make six figures.

In fact, I only need two to four clients per month to make multiple six figures in my business.

The key here is to focus on getting better clients, not more clients. More isn't necessarily better; better is better.

Consider the following questions when determining if a client is a good fit to work with:

- Can they afford you?
- Do they pay on time?
- Do they refer others to you?
- Do they communicate well, tell you what they want and need and not expect you to read their minds?

- Do they respect your expertise?
- Do they respect your time?

These are the types of clients you want to work with. I don't want to work with people who cannot afford me, aren't good communicators, don't respect my time or expertise and don't value my services.

George Carlin once said, "Anyone who drives slower than you is an idiot, and everyone who drives faster is a maniac."

Focus on working with people who are going your speed and you'll be much happier.

Sometimes when we are starting out in business, we are happy to get "any" paying client. I get that. But once you've been in business long enough, you realize you don't want just "any" client, you want to work with the best clients who are going your speed.

I once had a strategy session with a woman who told me she was going to "sell her car" to work with me.

I don't want anyone selling their means of transportation to get a book published and launched.

People at the high levels know they have to pay top dollar to get top service.

If you already have an existing business and you want to grow that business, raise your prices. Maybe even double or triple them.

I've had to do this several times in my business and the quality of people I work with now is phenomenal.

Does a high-maintenance, challenging client ever slip in?

Yes.

But I always deliver on my promises and then I make sure to take a mental note of how that happened and create more barriers to entry to working with me.

Weeding is a constant process, not a one-and-done event.

Also, when you charge premium prices for your services, you can hire other people and preserve your precious time for focusing on your strengths.

Now that we know it's best to go after the top 10% of the market – the high hanging fruit – and to charge premium prices, it's time to talk about hiring out your weaknesses so you can focus on your strengths.

Chapter 7:
Hire Out Your Weaknesses

One of the biggest mistakes I've made in my business is doing everything myself and believing that no one could do things better than I could.

I've learned now that successful entrepreneurs identify problems, discover the opportunities available to solving those problems, and then build systems that *allow other people and other things to get it done.*

In his book, *Virtual Freedom: How to Work With Virtual Staff to Buy More Time, Become More Productive, and Build Your Dream Business,* Author Chris Ducker says, "In late 2009, I found myself burnt out and stressed like never before. I woke up one day and realized something startling: I really didn't have a company. I was the company!"

If you remove "you" from your company and it can't operate without "you," then you really don't have a company.

Also, when you're doing every "thing" in your business, then you're not operating from your strengths; you're operating mostly from your weaknesses.

As my Bestselling Author Program was growing, I was staying up to wee hours of the morning/night editing and formatting books, designing book covers, and managing publishing projects from beginning to end.

Just like Chris Ducker, I was my company.

And guess what? I was working myself into a job. Because unfortunately, I was trading time for money once again.

I finally realized the error of my ways and fired myself from several specific roles that were better suited for other people.

My first hire was a Virtual Assistant to help me with the day-to-day operations of my business, and the second was an amazing editor and formatting assistant. These two hires saved my life and my business.

When you get burned out sometimes you think the only option is to shut things down. I admit, there were dozens of times I wanted to "quit" my business and I'm grateful I stuck with it and got through the "dip" and the hard times.

Deep down I loved books and I loved working with authors, I just didn't love doing ALL the work in my business.

During the time I was working with my business coach, he was NOT a fan of the "done-for-you" business model I had created. Most coaches are not doing done-for-you programs; it's more of a done-*with*-you program.

However, there was something deep inside of me that assured me the people who were my ideal clients (the ones short on time and high on cash) did not want to "learn" how to write, publish and launch a #1 bestselling book; they wanted me (and my team) to do it for them.

I stuck to that belief and today I have a very successful VIP done-for-you business that caters to high-end experts such as coaches, consultants, psychologists, speakers, trainers, doctors, lawyers, educators, and more.

Discover What You Don't Like Doing and Stop Doing It

Aside from the fact that one person cannot perform every role in a business without ending up burned out, stressed out and having a very unleveraged business – sometimes when you start a business you do perform more roles than you'd like to.

The key to long-term success, however, is to outsource your weaknesses as soon as you can afford to do so – and you need to do it sooner rather than later.

My mistake was waiting for years to make this shift.

Being a paralegal for 17 years, I was used to doing a lot of different tasks – some of them I loved and some of them I hated – but I did not have a choice.

I defaulted to this "suck it up" mentality and did everything in my business because it had become the *norm*. Also, I was lazy because I knew it was hard work to find, hire and train others in my business. What I didn't realize was the benefits would far outweigh the costs.

When I hired my publishing assistant to edit and format the books, it was like a weight was lifted off of my shoulders. It freed of more of my time to focus on things I was good at and that I loved like writing, selling and coaching.

Hiring Alex as my project manager was another great decision I made because he had the technology skills I needed to learn several aspects of my business quickly and to take a lot off of my plate.

Alex sets up book launches from start to finish, manages large publishing projects, proofreads books after they've been edited, creates and manages Amazon ads for clients, and sets up media interviews. He's even doing website maintenance for several websites.

He was doing such a phenomenal job, I decided to give him my "problem" clients. It's not that the "client" was a problem per se, it's just that these particular clients hired me months or even years ago, but never gave a manuscript. My program is a 12-week program so I called these clients my "stragglers." He's completed four of those projects, and I'm so happy he was able to take those off my plate.

I also noticed that every year I hired more people in my business that my income increases. So, my goal became to keep hiring people until I'm only working from my strengths.

According to Gallup research, only 20% of people are in a role where they have a chance to do what they do best every day using their strengths. Often in corporate America, you can't pick and choose your tasks if you want to keep your job.

That means 80% of the time people are not operating from their strengths. No wonder people hate their jobs.

In their book, First, *Break All The Rules: What the World's Greatest Managers Do Differently,* authors Marcus Buckingham and Curt Coffman say:

"You would be wise not to ignore your weaknesses. Great managers don't. As soon as they realize that a weakness is

causing the poor performance, they switch their approach. They know that there are only three possible routes to helping the person succeed. Devise a support system. Find a complementary partner. Or find an alternative role. Great managers quickly bear down, weigh these options and choose the best route."

When you have your own business, the stakes are even higher. If you're spending time on tasks and activities that are not your strengths, your business will most likely fail and you may end up broke.

I love the three options that great managers find as solutions for those employees whose weakness is causing poor performance:

1. Get support

2. Find a partner to help

3. Find an alternative role

As I said earlier, I kept firing myself and that is the key to achieving more success. I thought business was about learning and figuring out how to do everything in it, and now I see that the more your business operates without you, the more success your business will have.

In the book, *Work the System: The Simple Mechanics of Making More and Working Less*, by Sam Carpenter, he talks about his failing telecommunications business, Centratel, and says:

"For fifteen years Centratel struggled for survival, always at the brink of disaster. Why did this primary system begin to prosper in year sixteen? Yes, focused attention, terrific staff, targeted marketing, and a consistently high-quality

product went a long way, but they were not the cause of the turnaround. Instead, these were by-products of the cause. The reason for the turnaround was the discovery and application of the principle that leadership must focus on improving processes, not on performing the work OR on repeatedly snuffing out brushfires."

My business coach recommended this book to me and it changed my business and my life. It opened my eyes to creating systems.

In *Work the System* Sam Carpenter says:

"Your task is to optimize one system after another, not careen through the day randomly taking care of whatever problems erupt. Your job is not to be a fire killer. Your job is to prevent fires."

When you spend the majority of your time putting out fires, it's hard to change gears. It took some time to set up systems in my business, but now that they are set up, I have more free time.

The catch-22 is it takes time to set up the systems. My mentality had always been "it's quicker for me to just do it." And that's probably true in the short term, but I was doing the same repetitive tasks over and over and over which was not good use of my precious time. Every minute spent on things that weren't my strengths was taking time away from those things that are my strengths.

Sales is one of my core strengths. So when I was spending my time editing manuscripts or designing book covers, I was literally losing business.

It's interesting to me now, looking back, that my business made the same amount every year until I made this shift and then my income doubled and now it has tripled!

I think the best way to determine your strengths is to do the job autopsy I mentioned earlier. I go into great detail about job autopsies in my book *Quit Your Job and Follow Your Dreams: A 12-Month Guide to Being Joyfully Jobless.*

The main task of a job autopsy is to look at every job you've had and write down all the tasks involved in that particular job. Then, rate those tasks on a scale of 1-10 with the tasks you enjoyed the most rated the highest. Then, focus on the tasks which you rated 8s, 9s or 10s.

Statistics show that the most successful people create jobs where they spend a disproportionate amount of time doing what they love and it doesn't happen by accident.

In his book, *One Thing You Need to Know: About Great Managing, Great Leading, and Sustained Individual Success* author Marcus Buckingham says:

"Some people will tell you that it doesn't matter if you like your work; you just have to be good at it. Question this advice. You may well be good at some activities you don't enjoy, but your enjoyment is the fuel you require to keep practicing the activity, to keep stretching, investing and pushing yourself to greater levels of mastery. Lacking this enjoyment your performance will like plateau."

Writing is one of my strengths, and it is something I also enjoy and am passionate about. I know that are different schools of thoughts on this – some say just focus on what your good at whether you enjoy it or not – and others (like me and Marcus Buckingham) say that it's important for long-term success to be good at it and to enjoy it.

That's why I keep writing. It's not just because I'm good at it, it's because I truly love it.

What do you love so much that you would do even if you weren't being paid to do it?

Sometimes that's a good question to ask if you're stuck. If you've done the job autopsy exercise, you may have already figured out some of your strengths and things you truly enjoy.

Years ago I was teaching a workshop in Washington, D.C., and I asked the students to raise their hand if they loved sales. Only two people raised their hands out of dozens of people. That made me realize that majority of people hate selling. It's hard to be a successful entrepreneur if you're not good at selling and/or you don't like it.

It's all about self-knowledge and self-awareness. The better you know yourself, the more successful you will become.

Now that we've discussed hiring out your weaknesses, next up is the 6-Figure Blueprint and how you can start using it to create your own 6-figure business.

Chapter 8:
The 6-Figure Blueprint

I recently had a strategy session with a potential client for my Bestselling Author program. She asked me to look at her new website while we were on the call. The colors were vibrant and beautiful and the design was lovely, but I noticed there were no strong calls to action and I couldn't figure out what she was actually selling. Under the "Services" tab, I found:

- All Services
- Master Course
- Speaking and Seminars
- Soul Adventures
    - Clearing Process
    - The Journey
    - Coaching

There was no clear direction on her website and although she was talented, she wasn't able to convert visitors into paying customers.

As we talked more, I asked her what her main business was and she replied, "Coaching." When I asked her about the Master Course, I found out she spent enormous amounts of time and energy developing a course only to have a couple of people sign up for it.

Remember in an earlier chapter, we talked about launching fast and getting paying customers. Ideas are a dime a dozen. Until you actually have paying customers, you are wasting a lot of time.

This potential client was working on a book to grow her business and I told her to do that she needed to remove everything on her website under "services" and have one signature program. This way, the book and the signature program could work hand in hand.

She is an expert at what she does, highly credible, has a great title and hook for her book, but she was making the same mistake I made before I hired my business coach. She was selling a lot of programs and making a little bit of money on them instead of making a lot of money on fewer programs.

In fact, she was very interested in my program, but when I told her the cost, at first, she told me she couldn't afford it. She ended up moving some things around and did hire me and I'm so happy I can help her with her book and her website.

In this chapter, I'm going to share with you the 5-Step system that transformed my business from making $3-5k per month to making $20k-$50k+ per month.

Is it easy to execute?

No.

Execution is never easy because there is a learning curve and most things that are worthwhile and pay well are rarely easy. The fact is, most people will quit in the "dip" – the long slog where it gets really hard before you get to the mastery level.

Hopefully, you'll be one of the 20% of people who take action and implement what I'm about to teach you.

5-Step System:

1. Offer (one that is tested and converts)

2. Facebook Ad

3. Automated Webinar

4. Application

5. Phone Call

The Offer

I want to take you back to when I hired my business coach. I was just like the woman I mentioned above. On my Become a 6-Figure Woman Website, I was offering several online courses as well as coaching, website design, SEO, copywriting services and more. I was all over the place.

My coach told me to pick one thing to focus on while we built this automated system.

I chose the Bestselling Author online program because I already was selling this as a 6-week online course. After students completed the course, they asked me if I could just do it for them, and that's how my done-for-you program was born.

At first, I charged $1000 to get a previously published book to the bestsellers list. I got so many clients (high demand/low supply of my time) that I quickly increased my fee to $2000. I was still getting a lot of clients.

I began noticing that the quality of the books wasn't the best – the covers weren't very professional, the books were not properly edited, the book description was poorly written, and the hook was weak.

My coach said I needed a complete program that covered all of those elements as well as achieving best seller status. He recommended I create a program that took a mediocre book and turned it into a high-quality book that someone could use in their business and that's how my high-ticket done-for-you bestsellers program was created.

He suggested I charge $5000 for a 12-week done-for-you program. I thought he was crazy and said, "No one is going to pay $5000 for this." He said, "We'll see."

He was right and I was wrong.

The first month, I charged $3000 because I was afraid I wouldn't get clients at the $5k price point. That month, I signed up four new clients. My coach said, "Michelle, you just left $8000 ($2000 x 4 new clients) on the table. What could you and your family have done with $8000?"

Darn! He was right. If I had charged $5k like he told me, I would have had an extra $8k in my bank account that month. So, the next month I raised my price to $4k and, again, I had four people sign up. His comment to me this time was, "Michelle, you just left $4000 ($1000 x 4 new clients) on the table. What could you and your family have done with $4000?"

Darn! He was right again. The next month I listened to him and I had my first $20k+ month.

From the outside, I looked like I had one program, but I actually was selling a few different packages, but you couldn't tell that from my website. I learned not to publish packages or prices on your website without a phone call (strategy session).

So, Step 1 of the system is to have a proven offer that converts. I already had that, it was just that I was undercharging.

If you are creating something new, you want to test it out. It must solve a BIG problem in the marketplace that people are willing to pay top dollar for the high value.

I see a lot of life coaches sell generic programs like:

- Live an unstoppable life
- Live your best life
- Improve your life
- Level up your life

These are all very vague offers and most likely will not convert. To be successful, you need a specific offer. You need to tap into problems that keep people up at night, such as:

- My business is failing, and I need help fast
- My relationship is failing, and I need help fast
- My finances are failing, and I need help fast
- My health is failing, and I need help fast

The four big areas people need help with are:

1. money
2. business/career

3. relationships

4. health.

Focus on these.

Dan Kennedy, master copywriter and author of many books on direct marketing and sales, said in this book, *NO B.S. Direct Marketing:*

"Offer Services People WANT, Not What They Need."

Sell people what they want (or think they want) and then give them what they need once they are a client.

For example, in my publishing business, my clients want to become a bestselling author. That's the result they want so that's what I sell them. I'm not selling them "self-publishing" or "how to write a book."

When I work with my clients, however, I give them so much more. I give them a high-quality book and coach them on how they can leverage this bestselling book to achieve their goals. It's a 12-week done for you program.

If you have a program or service that is working and is proven, you can transform it into a high-level program.

Sometimes, you need to add some done-for-you elements, but you should never charge for your services by the hour. That's just making a job for yourself and this book is about getting out of the corporate grind and creating a 6-figure income working the least amount of time.

"Charge what the market will bear."

I was undercharging when I started out, and my prices have increased every year along with the quality and level of service I offer.

The minimum you should charge for a program that gets people the result they want in a specific period of time, ideally 8-12 weeks, should be $3000. Of course, when you're just starting out you can run a "BETA" program and offer it at a discount while you finalize the details.

My done-for-you program was originally offered at $1000. Once I saw how popular that service was, I developed it into the program I have now and increased the prices over time.

Remember, launch and learn quickly.

Don't make the mistake of not charging enough because then you will start attracting Group 1 – those with an abundance of time, but no money. This group of people can be very draining and burdensome. They are typically the shiny object chasers who don't want to do the hard work and follow things to execution. Make sure you're charging enough to attract the VIP people in Group 2.

People pay top dollar for transformation, not information.

Your offer should provide a transformation, not only information.

Here are some examples of very specific offers:

- Scale your business in 90 days
- Discover a traffic system that can turn $1 into $3, $4, $5 or more on an ongoing basis

- How to Build a Business That Gives You a Freedom Lifestyle in two years or Less

- Break up Coaching: Survive Your soul-crushing breakup. Bounce back with understanding, insight and self-worth.

- Become an Irresistible Catch to an Irreplaceable Partner of the Opposite Sex

Facebook Ads

I started running Facebook ads in 2015 and stopped running them at the end of 2017 because I had more business than I could handle! Now, I get all of my business from referrals. I pay a commission to anyone who refers business to me.

I am by no means an expert at Facebook ads. Facebook ads is NOT an easy platform for beginners, and you may need support which I'll talk about more later.

This section provides an overview of the ads that I ran for my business during this time which grew my business exponentially and were an important piece of my 6-figure success.

There are other types of paid advertising that works well such as YouTube ads, LinkedIn ads, and more. My coach once told me, "If you don't have paid traffic getting you clients, you don't have a business." Remember that.

History of My Facebook Ads

Before I created my automated webinar in 2017, I ran an ad that directed Facebook traffic to my "Case Studies Page" on my website.

My First Ad

(That was me before my hair turned white! lol)

I call this my "beginners ad." It wasn't terrible, and it did get me strategy sessions, but in today's savvy social media world, I don't think this ad would work very well. But everyone has to start somewhere, and this is where I started.

Clicking on the "Learn More" button on the ad above took visitors to my website where I presented six case studies.

This beginner ad worked for a while as I was busy developing my program, increasing my package prices, and creating my automated webinar.

It was not easy getting my webinar finalized. The biggest obstacle I faced was that I was "over-teaching" in my webinar. Thankfully, my coach kept correcting me, and then I would redo the webinar. It took several months to get it right.

We will talk below about the content of the webinar, but the rule of thumb is "Teach them the what, but not the how."

A webinar is a sales tool, not a training session detailing everything you know about a topic. I'm a natural teacher, so I would try to teach way too much on each slide. The webinar was too long and probably would not get me strategy sessions.

It's a tough line to follow – to just tell people about your topic and not how to solve their problem.

Okay, getting back to the Facebook ads…

My Second Ad

 Like   Comment   Share   Buffer

On Facebook, it's important to test each of the following parts of your ad to create a "winning ad."

- Images
- Headline
- Call To Action

When you put all the winning parts together, then you have a winning ad!

I tested three images to get the winner.

Below are the other two images that did NOT convert:

I have to tell you I got very attached to images I found that I thought would work. My coach kept saying, "It doesn't matter whether you love or hate the image, the data will tell us what works."

Data outweighs your opinion.

What matters is what appeals to prospects and what image they click on, not what you like. So keep that in mind as you choose images – don't get too attached!

Always test three images.

My first Facebook ad included a photo of myself, but I would not recommend doing that unless you are famous. People are not on Facebook to see ads, they are there for social reasons. If they see your photo with ad copy around it, they will *know* it's an ad and most likely will ignore it.

Select vibrant photos that make people HAPPY. Beach pictures do well and interestingly, sunflowers, always do well.

At the time, the ad above with the starfish was the winning ad because we tested the image, the headline, and the call to action. Then, we ran this ad for a few months to three different target groups.

*Detailed targeting is a feature available with Facebook ads that allows you target very specific demographics such as age, gender, income, marital status, interests, and more.

My Targeting for This Ad

1. Writers/Authors as follows: Writer's Digest, Association of Writers & Writing Programs, The Writer's Circle, AuthorHouse, Amazon Kindle Direct Publishing, CreateSpace or IBooks Author, Field of study: Creative Writing, Job title: Published Author or Penulis; **REACH – 300,000** (I named this **campaign "Writers"**)

2. Business Coaches, Career Coaches, Certified Health Coaches, Certified Trainers, Executive Coaches, Executive Consultant, Health and Wellness Coach, Health Coach, Health Consultant, Health/Wellness Consultant, Life Coach, Life Coaching, Life Skills Coach, Motivational Speaker, Nutritionist, Performance Coach, Personal Coach, Personal Development Mentor, Personal Wellness Coach, Public Speaking, Sales Coach, Speaker, Success Coach, Trainer/Coach, Wellness Advocate/Consultant, Wellness Coach (I named these *Coaches*); **REACH – 21,000 ;**

3. Ali Brown, Bill Barne, Fabienne Fredrickson, Female Entrepreneur Association, Frank Kern,

Kevin Nations, Lisa Sasevich, Marie Forleo, Mike Koenigs (I called this *Gurus*); **REACH – 390,000**

NOTE: In September 2017, Facebook made an update that no longer allows you to target "job titles." So, the ads I previously had that targeted anyone who had "writer or author or coach" in their title would no longer be allowed. To work around this limitation, find associations in which a specific job title belongs and use those in your ads.

For example, if I want to target my ads to writers, then I can use the Non-Fiction Writer's Association (or any other writer's groups) in my ad. This will require you to do some research when setting up your ads.

Okay, getting back to the ads I was running…

My detailed targeting included:

- Homeowners
- Age 30-60
- Both men and women
- English language only
- US only
- Income ranges:
    - $75,000-99,000
    - $100,000 to 124,999
    - $125,000 - 149,000
    - $150,000 – 249,000
    - $350,000 – 499,999
    - over $500,000
- Desktop and mobile.
- Feeds
- Traffic destination: website

- I ran for Link Clicks and did Automatic bidding.
- $10 per day spending on these ads.
- Buying type: Auction

The starfish ad "fatigued" after a while and the price per click increased. So, we paused that ad. I copied the text and added a new image and ran this new ad:

This image above had the best conversions and I know that because we tested it! In fact, I loved this image so much, when I designed my new website, I used it on the home page: www.bestsellingauthorprogram.com

For this ad, I increased the budget to $22.00 per day and ran it to the GURU's Group:

Ali Brown, Bill Barne, Fabienne Fredrickson, Female Entrepreneur Association, Frank Kern, Kevin Nations, Lisa Sasevich, Marie Forleo, Mike Koenigs

As I mentioned, we tested three images before we came up with the one in this ad.

Below is another image that did **NOT** convert:

6 Figure Woman
Sponsored · 🌐   👍 Like Page

Want to Become a #1 Bestselling Author and Boost Your Brand, Business and Visibility? There's a secret "Backwards Book Launch" method that allows you to increase your profits.

Free Training Reveals my Proven "Backwards Book Launch" Formula for Becoming a #1 Bestselling Author

Discover the 3 Reasons Why You Absolutely Must Become a #1 Bestselling Author with my secret "Backwards Book Launch" method and how to make bigger profits...

ONLINEMEETINGNOW.COM

👍 Like   💬 Comment   ↪ Share   ≋ Buffer

The winning ad that was working fatigued after a while so we copied it and tested new ad copy (using the same image with three different ad copies) and ran it to the same gurus group at $22 per day split up between the three ads:

Ad #1:

Ad #2:

Ad #3 – The Winner!

6 Figure Woman
Sponsored · 🌐

👍 **Like Page**

Imagine becoming a #1 Bestselling Author in the next 30-60 days.

What would your business look like if you were the go-to expert in your niche' and people were lining up to be your client?

Being a #1 bestselling author immediately turns YOU into an expert in your market.

Free Training: How to Become a #1 Bestselling Author Using The Secret "Backwards Book Launch" Formula.

Discover how to write a bestselling book that can double and triple your income and the #1 reason why must become a #1 bestselling author now.

ONLINEMEETINGNOW.COM

So, Facebook ads is all about TESTING! And to TEST, you have to spend money.

I recommend a minimum of $10 a day to start and then increase your budget when you have a winning ad. Run the ad for about 4-7 days to see which one is the winner.

To select the winner, you should track the following numbers:

- Click through rate of 1% or higher (how many people are clicking on your ad)

- Relevancy score of 3 or higher (how relevant your ad is to the audience)

- Frequency rate under 2 (how often FB shows the ad)

Get Started Running Facebook Ads and Automated Webinar Funnel:

The System:

1. The first step in this "process" is to bring cold traffic in through the top of your funnel (your webinar). It's very important to start this process by split testing at least 3-5 different audiences. When I began, I tested audiences of "writers/authors," "coaches," and "gurus" – and the winner was "gurus."

2. Your ad spend during this testing phase should be no less than $10 per day per audience.

3. Drive these audiences to a landing page where they can register for your webinar. I used Leadpages for my landing page.

NOTE: A healthy cost per registration is about $2.50, however, this is only one piece of the puzzle. Depending on the market it can be $5-$10 per registration, BUT as long as you are getting a high ROI on your ad spend, and converting them into sales, that's okay. My average cost per click is between $3 and $4 typically; my average cost per registration was about $14.)

The Tools

- I used Stealth to run my automated webinar because they will set everything up for you. There is a $97 setup fee and then $67 per month after that. Here is the link to connect with them: http://www.stealthseminar.com/

Using an automated webinar platform has *huge* benefits. The system is designed to nurture your registrants with reminder emails and follow up emails which makes the process super easy for you...and that is what we want, *right?*

Evergreen Webinars

An Evergreen Webinar is a webinar you can run over and over and over.

The goal of the webinar funnel is to drive COLD traffic through Facebook ads so people can register for your automated webinar.

What are most people doing in these webinar trainings?

These webinars provide a ton of value and end with a sales pitch for their product, service, course or event.

I wasn't selling anything, but instead I offered a strategy session with me at the end of my webinar.

TIPS:

- Most people know that you're going to pitch your product at the end of your webinar, so they leave before it's over. Offer a FREE gift at the conclusion of the webinar for those who stay until the end (of course, you want to mention this at the beginning of your webinar).

- Some prospects who were potentially interested will not stay for the entire webinar.

- Others will register but not show up.

None of the above circumstances necessarily means the people who registered for your webinar aren't the right prospects; it just means that life happened and they may need some time to convert, or it will take a different path to convert.

Ideally, you want people to sign up and convert on the spot, but it doesn't always happen right away.

It's great to get multiple webinar registrations, but the majority of conversions happen through retargeting.

The Retargeting Process

As soon as a lead registers for the event/webinar/training, they are immediately put into a website traffic custom audience funnel based on which confirmation page they were on when registering for the webinar.

To successfully organize your leads, you must have your pixel set up properly on your website. Stealth will put your custom conversion pixel on the thank you or confirmation page for you.

Once the segments are properly set up, and leads register for the event, I can send out specific ads to just those people.

Now, you're probably wondering, what type of ads do I send them?

I'm glad you asked.

I immediately send them ads that directly pitch the offer I talk about on the webinar itself.

This is such a powerful and useful tool to bring in sales or strategy sessions over and over.

Remember, these were cold leads which means more time is often needed to convert. Because they weren't quite ready during the webinar, doesn't mean they are not your ideal audience and that they're not going to buy at some point.

In conclusion, this simple but incredibly powerful Facebook Ads Funnel consists of:

- Testing images, headlines and calls to action
- Split testing 3-5 audiences to find your best audience.
- Filling your value-packed webinar using traffic from Facebook Ads that target cold traffic
- Making the offer on the webinar itself (strategy or discovery session)
- Retargeting those registrants with ads promoting your offer

All you need is two ad campaigns — one to grab the cold leads for the funnel, and one to retarget with them with your offer once they've registered.

This is truly one of the simplest yet most effective funnels out there.

Questions to answer when creating your ads and campaign:

1. What are three things your clients struggle with? For example, in my market, clients are struggling with how to become a #1 bestselling author, how to make money from their book, and how to become the go-to expert in their market with a book. Write the three struggles your clients are having below.

   _____

   _____

   _____

   _____

   _____

   _____

   *You are going to turn these struggles into a pain point statement or question that leads into your Facebook ad. For example, in one of my ads I say, "Imagine becoming a #1 Bestselling Author in the next 30-60 days; What would your business look like if you were the go-to expert in your niche' and people were lining up to be your client; Being a #1 bestselling author immediately turns YOU into an expert in your market." OR I could have said, "Struggling to become a #1 bestselling Author?"

2. Take your ideas above and turn them into a statement or a question below:

_____

_____

_____

_____

_____

_____

List three benefits that anyone who purchases your program or service will receive:

_____

_____

_____

_____

3. What images represent your offer? I use water and beach scenes and they seem to work well. Other people use graphics made with Canva or Picmonkey. What images would work well in your niche'?

_____

_____

_____

_____

_____

_____

_____

4. It's very important to do this research before you set up your ad. Who does your ideal client "follow" and "like" that are similar to you? List 10 pages, groups or people here:

_____

_____

_____

_____

_____

_____

_____

_____

_____

_____

_____

5. What is the BIG goal you have for your Facebook ad – to grow your list, create brand awareness, schedule strategy sessions, or sell a product?

_____

_____

_____

_____

_____

_____

_____

_____

_____

Answer the questions above and then design your ad using this template:

Text (words above the image): Want to Become a #1 Bestselling Author and Boost Your Brand, Business and Visibility? There's a secret "Backwards Book Launch" method that allows you to increase your profits. **THINK: What result is the potential client is looking for or what pain point are they having?**

Headline (directly below the image): Free Training Reveals my Guaranteed and Proven "Backwards Book Launch" Formula for Becoming a #1 Bestselling Author. **EXAMPLE: FREE Training, FREE ebook, or FREE Masterclass about some topic or twist on a topic they haven't heard of before.**

Description (below the image): "Discover the 3 Reasons Why You Absolutely Must Become a #1 Bestselling Author with my secret *Backwards Book Launch* method and how to make bigger profits from your book. **THINK: What will they discover by clicking on your offer and what will be the BIG benefit?**

6 Figure Woman
Sponsored · 🌐

Want to Become a #1 Bestselling Author and Boost Your Brand, Business and Visibility? There's a secret "Backwards Book Launch" method that allows you to increase your profits.

Free Training Reveals my Proven "Backwards Book Launch" Formula for Becoming a #1 Bestselling Author

Discover the 3 Reasons Why You Absolutely Must Become a #1 Bestselling Author with my secret "Backwards Book Launch" method and how to make bigger...

ONLINEMEETINGNOW.COM

👍❤ 25   1 Comment 11 Shares

👍 Like   💬 Comment   ➦ Share   ⪢ Buffer

Once your ad is designed, you need to do the following:

1. Put the pixel on your website

2. If doing the webinar funnel, put a custom conversion pixel on the confirmation page of the webinar

3. Create a campaign (Purpose of the ad)

4. Create the ad set (who you want your ad shown to and how)

5. Create three ads and test them.

6. Run the winning ad for a week or so and check the stats every day or every other day.

7. Continue running that ad as long as the numbers are good.

8. Pause the ad at any time the numbers aren't ideal.

9. Once the ad fatigues, create a new ad.

10. I recommend getting Facebook Ads training or hiring a Facebook Ads Coach or Company to set this up properly.

I worked with my coach for a year before we had this funnel set up, but remember, I already had an offer that was and proven and that converted which was my bestselling author program.

Do NOT run Facebook ads unless you have the same.

How to get automated webinar up and running:

1. Create Webinar slides in PowerPoint or Keynote.

2. Record the webinar (45-60 minutes max); I recorded mine using a free/low-cost program called screen-cast-o-matic.

   a. Upload to Stealth via their Webinar Encoder

3. Record a 3½ minute **Confirmation Page Video** that attendees will be redirected to once they sign up for your webinar (this increases the show up rate exponentially and is highly recommended).

4. Upload the Confirmation Video to **YouTube**.

   a. Copy the link because you will need that for Stealth.

5. Create your Webinar Registration Page in Lead Pages

    a. Stealth will duplicate this page so don't worry about the Integration settings. Copy the link to send to Stealth.

6. Create your **Strategy Session Application** page using Gravity Forms

    a. Note: If you already have a strategy session application on your website and navigation bar, do not use that one. Create a new page with no navigation bar – only the form – to be used by people who register for the webinar that come from Facebook ads. *I bought the domain www.bestsellerchat.com and I use this to redirect leads from the automated webinar via Facebook ads to the strategy session application . So, bestsellerchat.com redirects to: http://bestsellingauthorprogram.com/apply/

7. Create a new list in Aweber or have Stealth create it.

    a. Call the list "Webinar Leads" or something similar

    b. Send that list to Stealth so they can have webinar registrants added to your list

8. **Write Symptom-Based Emails** and put them in your Webinar Leads Autoresponder series. Start with a few and add to them. Schedule one email to go out daily, but do not send out until day 2 or 3 because they are already getting follow-up messages from Stealth with the replay. *** Please note that Stealth will set up their

own webinar follow-up email reminders to people that register for the webinar so you don't have to do that. *A Symptom-Based email addresses the pain points your prospective clients have.*

9. **Submit a support ticket to Stealth** to have your webinar set up. Stealth will provide a link you can use to submit everything needed to them, including

   a. The name of the Webinar you want to use (in case you have more than one).

   b. A link to the confirmation page YouTube video.

   c. The Leadpages registration page link for the webinar.

   d. The link to the Strategy Session Application.

   e. The Aweber account details and list (or whatever email system you use).

   f. The **Button** you want to use for your **CALL TO ACTION**. Watch your webinar and make note of when you start talking about signing up for a strategy session. For example, if your webinar is 50 minutes long, and you land on the final page where you share the link to sign up for a call with you at the 40-minute mark, then you need to tell Stealth to insert your Call to Action Button at the 40-minute mark.

Notes About Stealth

- Use the "Just In Time" Top of the hour setting for your webinar to play. My webinar played from 9 a.m. EST to 9 p.m. EST *This does cause a problem for other countries, but currently I am only running the ads to the US market.

- Disable chat replay

This summarizes the Offer to Facebook Ads to an automated Webinar to the Application Page and finally to a Strategy Session.

Now, I want to talk about the Automated Webinar content, the Strategy Session Application and the Strategy Session itself.

Automated Webinar *Content*

As I mentioned, I struggled creating the content and slides for my webinar because I was over-teaching. I think this is a common problem creators have because we have so much knowledge we want to share with the world. When you over-teach, you make it hard for people to follow because they are going to be on information overload.

Two ways to overcome this common problem.

First, teach the "Top 5 Mistakes" or whatever number you can come up with. So, I could do my webinar on "The Top 5 Mistakes Authors Make When Publishing a Book." That's a great title and it's curiosity-driven which is what you want. If you're an aspiring author, then you would want to know what those mistakes are, right?

Think about your niche' and the mistakes you've made or the people you've worked with have made. Make those mistakes the topic of your automated webinar. It's very powerful and this will prevent you from over-teaching on your topic.

Another method that works well is to "Teach the What, but NOT the How." In my bestselling author program, I created a webinar titled: "3 Steps to Becoming a Bestselling Author" and on it, I taught the what, but not the how.

For example one of the steps to becoming a bestselling author is selecting the right categories and keywords for your book. I explain that this is a part of the process and why it's important, but I don't go into the details on "how" to select the categories and keywords.

My webinar would be 6 hours long if I taught all the details on this topic! You cannot teach everything you know and you should not try to.

Remember, the webinar is a tool designed to get you strategy sessions so you can sell your program. It's not for you to teach everything you know or to prove how smart you are. You will not be teaching on the strategy session call either. The purpose of the strategy call is to find out if your solution is the best option for the problems your prospect is having.

The length of your webinar should be based on the type of clients you are trying to attract. If you're going for high-ticket clients, the webinar should be 20-40 minutes long as they are short on time and high on cash. If you are trying to attract lower-ticket clients, your webinar can be 60 minutes or longer. For reference, a high-ticket client will spend $3000 or more and a low-ticket will spend less than $2000.

Create PowerPoint or Keynote slides for your webinar so you can follow along and not leave anything out. You don't want to sound rehearsed, you want to be yourself. You can have notes for each slide when you're recording your webinar that attendees don't see.

I really struggled with designing the slides. I let that slow me down a lot as I spent an inordinate amount of time selecting the images and writing the copy for each slide. I don't recommend doing what I did.

To make it simple, you could have a white background with some black font and no colors or images and still make six figures. I see it done all the time.

I often included too much copy on the slides and then had to remove the majority of it. People don't want to read slides with multiple lines of text. List the major talking points on the slide (think headlines), but do not write everything you are going to say word for word.

I'm an introvert, so I think a lot of my procrastination was a result of my fear of being seen. I don't really like doing videos. I prefer the written word, however, I knew that a webinar would be a great way to get new clients so I stepped out of my comfort zone and did it.

Next up is the application page.

APPLICATION

At the end of your webinar, you are not selling anything. What you are offering is an opportunity to set up a strategy call with you. It's brilliant really. No hard sell, let's just get on a call and have a chat.

Take a look at my strategy session application at:

http://bestsellingauthorprogram.com/coaching/

Of course you want to collect the basic information about the person like name, email, phone, website address, country. Then, ask questions like:

- What is the biggest obstacle holding you back regarding _____ (your topic)?
- What is your goal regarding (this topic)?
- Why have you reached out to me at this time?
- What are you struggling with right now?
- What is your target income?

Ask any other questions that will give you more insight into their problems, obstacles, struggles, desired goals, and reasons why they are reaching out to you.

To weed out leads that are not qualified, ask a question similar to this one at the end of it:

"Are you looking for an experienced mentor to ensure your book is done right and to help you achieve your dreams of becoming a #1 Amazon Bestselling author?

- **Yes - I invest in myself often and get massive returns on my investments.**

- **Maybe - I haven't done this before but I am committed to being a #1 Amazon Bestselling Author!**

- **No - I am not able to invest in myself right now, but please send me any free information you have."**

Don't schedule a call with anyone who answers No. Review the answers from anyone who says maybe and send them an email with additional follow-up questions before scheduling a call.

Strategy Session (Phone Call)

Selling from a sales page on a website is hard. It is much easier to sell on a phone call (as long as you don't fear asking for what you're worth). I've found that a personal phone call is the best way to get new clients. On a strategy session, listen to the prospect talk about some of their challenges and problems, then share a personal story or two. If it's a good fit, invite them to join your program.

When you invite them to join, don't go over all the details of your program, such as:

- I have 24 video tutorials

- I have 100 PDFs, and assessments and quizzes

- I have workbooks or manuals

Don't sell the details of what the program contains, just sell the solution – which is YOU!

Also remember, the point of the call is not to "teach, train or coach." You want to determine what this person is struggling with to see if you can help them.

I use an automated scheduling software to book my calls, so the process goes like this:

- They land on my strategy session application either through a google search or an automated webinar and they fill it out.

- Once they hit submit, they are redirected to my scheduling software. I use **OnceHub**.

- If an appointment comes through that is not qualified, I cancel it and email the lead. Otherwise, I do the call on the scheduled day.

- I sign up 50-75% of people I talk to once they are qualified. I have a unique program that offers high value and high engagement which is what people are looking for.

Next up is an important topic about overcoming underearning and charging what you're worth!

Chapter 9:
Overcoming Underearning

In her book, *Money, A Memoir: Women, Emotions and Cash*, author Liz Perle says:

"Whether we want to admit it or not, each of us has a relationship to money that goes beyond the getting and spending. Money is never just money; it's our proxy for identity and love and hope and promises made and perhaps never fulfilled. It's our social sorter. It's the ticket to our dreams."

Whether we want to admit it or not, we need money to achieve our big dreams and goals.

Unfortunately, women are chronic underearners and one of the challenges is that we often were raised and taught to be kind, nurturing, cooperative and collaborative. Therefore, our roles revolve more around relationships, than money.

Men, on the other hand, use money as a differentiator and society sizes them up by how much they earn. Men rank their self-esteem by their productivity in the world as well as how successful they are because they are raised this way.

Don't misunderstand the term "underearners." They are often NOT lazy people in any way. In fact, they are almost always the hardest working people usually having multiple jobs, working long hours, and volunteering at non-profits, etc.

Karen McCall, author of *Financial Recovery: Developing a Healthy Relationship With Money*, describes an underearner as:

"Underearners compromise their financial circumstances by accepting less for their work than it is worth, and often less than they need to live the way they want and deserve to. They commonly have difficulty setting limits, saying no, or asking for what they need and deserve..."

So where does this underearning come from?

Not from a lack of intelligence or hard work, it comes from something much deeper – a profound sense of deprivation and shame.

Deprivation comes from our unmet needs, and in order to fill those needs we have to be honest about them. When you live in a state of deprivation, you are living in a state of emptiness and longing. This often happens when our physical, emotional, social or spiritual needs are not met early in life.

Deprivation often turns into self-neglect, overindulgence, addictions, helplessness, compulsions, and taking care of others at the expense of our own wellbeing.

The first step to healing these emotional wounds is acknowledging that you have them which helps you become more aware about them.

The next step is learning how to meet your needs and eliminating that deprivation mentality.

In the book, *Earn What You Deserve,* by Jerold Mudis, he defines underearning this way:

"...to repeatedly gain less income than you need, or than would be beneficial, usually for no apparent reason and despite your desire to do otherwise."

So, if you are an underearner, you are probably bringing in much less than you could be and have a lot of excuses as to why that is happening.

Author, Barbara Stanny, who has written numerous books on money, women, and power, writes in her book *"Secrets of Six-Figure Women"* about the 9 Traits of Underearners which are:

1. *Underearners have a high tolerance for low pay.*

2. *Underearners underestimate their worth.*

3. *Underearners are willing to work for free.*

4. *Underearners are lousy negotiators.*

5. *Underearners practice reverse snobbery.*

6. *Underearners believe in the nobility of poverty.*

7. *Underearners are subtle self-saboteurs.*

8. *Underearners are unequivocally codependent.*

9. *Underearners live in financial chaos.*

I included this chapter to make you aware that although you might say you want to make six figures, if you are an underearner, you are probably going to self-sabotage yourself, undercharge, and not achieve your income goals.

If you continually find yourself in financial crisis, you probably are an underearner.

For many years, I was an underearner and I had to do a lot of therapy, read many books on the subject, and work on myself-worth to overcome being an underearner.

The crazy part is you could actually be making six figures and still be an underearner. Either you are capable of making much more, or you are still living in financial chaos.

Therefore, it's not about the income level you are at, but about the nine traits mentioned above.

I would recommend reading any of Barbara Stanny's books on this topic. I also love Karen McCall's book as well as a book by Deborah Price titled *Money Magic* in which she says: ***"Money is a tool meant to help transform your life in more meaningful ways."***

I love that!

You absolutely have the power within you to manifest everything that you desire and the power to evolve and make a difference in the world. To do that, we have to step away from the anxiety, fears, and shame we feel about money.

I want you to have everything you desire and to step into your power around money.

When I first started making six figures in 2004, I felt somewhat guilty that I was making more money than my parents and most of my friends. Eventually, I realized my faulty thinking and now I see that money helps me provide for myself and my family, have fun experiences, go to cool places, enjoy life, and share my gifts with the world.

If I was still stuck in my 9-to-5 job living paycheck to paycheck, I would not be writing this book or living in my beautiful house on the water or working only 20-25 hours per week earning multiple six figures.

When you grow and evolve, so does your income. If you're stagnant in your financial life, you're probably stagnant in other areas.

If you want to take a money assessment test and find out what kind of money archetype you resonate with, go to Deborah Prices website at:

www.moneycoachinginstitute.com/money-type-quiz/

The eight money types are:

1. The Innocent

2. The Victim

3. The Warrior

4. The Martyr

5. The Fool

6. Creator/Artist

7. The Tyrant

8. The Magician

I am a money magician and proud of it! Magicians know how to transform and manifest their own financial reality and claim their power.

It's been a long road to get here, and I want the same for you.

It may take a little work, but you deserve financial prosperity, wealth, and to enjoy your life with all the desires of your heart.

Next we are going to talk about the art of making multiple six figures.

Chapter 10:
Creating Multiple 6-Figures

The goal is to generate the most amount of money in the least amount of time. M*ore* money buys you *more* freedom and *more* options.

Mike Michaelowicz, the author of *Profit First: Transform Your Business from a Cash-Eating Monster to a Money-Making Machine*, says:

"Without enough money, we cannot fully realize our authentic selves. Money amplifies who we are. There isn't a single ounce of doubt in my mind that there is something BIG you are intended to do on this planet. You wear the cape of what I believe is the greatest of all superheroes: the Entrepreneur. But your superhero powers can only yield as much power as your energy source provides. Money. You need money, superhero."

Just imagine the BIG things you could do with a multiple six-figure income and the impact you could make changing the world and leaving a legacy.

You don't have to create a huge company with hundreds of employees. I believe the perfect size for your business will happen naturally.

Earning six figures is a great and worthy goal to achieve; and once you get there, the next goal, if it feels right, should be multiple six figures.

Once you've made your first six figures, you can usually find new income streams that complement your main business.

The best part of making multiple six figures is that it allows me to be very selective with whom I work with in my business. I don't have to take on the wrong clients or projects that are out of my wheelhouse just to generate income.

Below are some case studies of entrepreneurs who have taken successful 6-figure businesses to multiple six figures and even seven figures.

CASE STUDY #1:

Brooke Castille, Founder of The Life Coach School, went from making six figures to multiple six figures, and now she is making multi-millions.

She started her business doing individual coaching, then added group coaching. Once she had a successful six-figure business, she began certifying others in her coaching methodology because she was getting more clients than she could help.

CASE STUDY #2

Mike Michaelowicz, author of *Profit First*, also has a certification program that allows others to become a "Profit First Professional" certified coach.

Instead of thinking small and only working with clients that come to him from his bestselling book, instead, Mike created a certification program and certifies accountants, bookkeepers, financial planners, business coaches and more in his methodology. He generates seven figures from his certification business!

CASE STUDY #3

Me! For years I made six figures and last year I added another 6-figure stream of income related to my main business.

I am now able to get client's books to the Wall Street Journal and USA Today Bestsellers lists in addition to the Amazon bestsellers list.

It sort of happened by accident, but when I saw the opportunity, I knew it would be transformative for my business and for my clients.

My core business is helping clients publish high-quality books that have an important message and then launching those books to #1 on the Amazon bestsellers list.

In 2018, I had a multi-millionaire client that wanted to be a Wall Street Journal and USA Today bestselling author. At the time, I had no idea how those lists worked. I did some research, found the criteria required to hit those lists, and partnered with a successful author whose business books have all hit those lists.

We put together a high-ticket program and with just three clients, I now have an additional 6-figure stream of income!

I've learned there will always be clients who want the next level higher than what you are offering. If what you are offering is already high-ticket, then they want high-high-ticket!

Some ways to create additional streams of income:

- If your core program is an 8-12-week program, consider adding a recurring monthly coaching program for $1k-$3k per month.
- Add on an exclusive in-person training or event
- License your materials
- Create a certification program
- Write a book

I think writing a book is one of the best investments you can make because a book can attract new clients. So, if you have a $5k or $10k+ program, just a few clients per month from your book can generate thousands of dollars in income.

My goal for 2020 is to write a book each month, and by 2021, I want to be generating six figures in passive income solely from my book royalties on Amazon.

Is it easy to write a book a month?

No!

However, I read a blog post that said the average 6-figure author has 22-28 books published, so last year I decided I wanted to earn six figures as an author and writer.

I love writing, and I love that people now want to read shorter books. Amazon has an entire category of books called "Short Reads," so I don't have to write books that are hundreds of pages long. I can focus on short reads and aim for 100-125 page books.

In December 2019, I published and launched *Quit Your Job and Follow Your Dreams;* in January 2020, I published and launched *How to Find Your Passion: 23 Questions that Can Change Your Life,* and in February 2020, this book is being published. Then, every month after that, I will rinse and repeat.

Every three books I write will be grouped as a series, and I will also create a box set which gives me another product to sell on Amazon. At the end of the year, I'll not only have 12 more new published books in addition to the 10 books I currently have on Amazon, but I'll have four box sets, too!

Hopefully, in January 2021, I'll be writing a book called ***"How to Write a Book a Month and Generate Six Figures"***! I love to teach what I learn and show others how they can achieve the same results I have.

If you're just starting out, keep all of this information in the back of your mind. I promise you opportunities will present themselves once you make your first six figures.

And now for my Closing Thoughts....

Closing Thoughts

When you have more money than you need, that's WEALTH. When you use your money to make a difference in the world, that's POWER.

Money is power. Money is influence. Money is freedom. Money is options. Money is impact. Money is flow. Money is opportunity.

Once you become financially secure from making six figures, you can use your money to make your mark. Look for opportunities and ways to gain more influence, have an impact, and to give back to others.

Don't let obstacles stand in the way of your dreams.

In his book, *The Obstacle is the Way: The Timeless Art of Turning Trials into Triumph,* author Ryan Holiday says:

"The struggle against an obstacle inevitably propels the fighter to a new level of functioning. The extent of the struggle determines the extent of the growth. The obstacles is an advantage, not adversity. The enemy is any perception that prevents us from seeing this."

Wherever you are on this path, you are going to face obstacles. Embedded in these obstacles are jewels of wisdom and benefits that are only for you.

Adversity is always waiting to be transformed into an advantage.

When I was fired from my job at the law firm, with no money in the bank and three young children to support, I had no idea what I was going to do.

Getting fired was the best thing that ever happened to me. It led me down a new path, one where I was able to create my own freedom and generate a 6-figure income without a boss, commute, or job.

Don't allow the obstacles on your path right now stop you from achieving your dreams.

The book *A Course in Miracles reminds us: "You do not ask too much of life but far too little."*

Stuart Wilde, one of my favorite authors, talks about how money is just energy in motion.

In his book, *The Trick to Money Is Having Some*, he says:

"The reason why money is such a JOY is that it allows you to grow spiritually, to understand the finer subtleties of life and to come to grips with many aspects of yourself."

Money will empower you, empower others, set you free, and make the world a better place.

I want you to DREAM BIG and never, ever give up on your dreams. Understand that the obstacles are the way to everything you desire.

I want to leave you with this affirmation which you can repeat to yourself daily: *"I am always in the right place at the right time. Abundance is simple and natural to me, all of my needs are constantly met."*

Would you do me a favor?

Reviews are so important on Amazon. If you loved this book and found it helped you, will you share your thoughts in a review on Amazon?

Thank you so much for reading, I truly appreciate it!

With much Love and Gratitude,

Michelle Kulp, 2020

Printed in Great Britain
by Amazon

35689935R00069